Sheriff

Morgan Brody

EZ READERS

Creating Young Nonfiction Readers

EZ Readers lets children delve into nonfiction at beginning reading levels. Young readers are introduced to new concepts, facts, ideas, and vocabulary.

Tips for Reading Nonfiction with Beginning Readers

Talk about Nonfiction
Begin by explaining that nonfiction books give us information that is true. The book will be organized around a specific topic or idea, and we may learn new facts through reading.

Look at the Parts
Most nonfiction books have helpful features. Our *EZ Readers* include a Contents page, an index, a picture glossary, and color photographs. Share the purpose of these features with your reader.

Contents
Located at the front of a book, the Contents displays a list of the big ideas within the book and where to find them.

Index
An index is an alphabetical list of topics and the page numbers where they are found.

Picture Glossary
Located at the back of the book, a picture glossary contains key words/phrases that are related to the topic.

Photos/Charts
A lot of information can be found by "reading" the charts and photos found within nonfiction text. Help your reader learn more about the different ways information can be displayed.

With a little help and guidance about reading nonfiction, you can feel good about introducing a young reader to the world of *EZ Readers* nonfiction books.

Printing 1 2 3 4 5 6 7 8 9

Author: Morgan Brody
Designer: Ed Morgan
Editor: Sharon F. Dorasamy

Names/credits:
Title: Sheriff / by Morgan Brody
Description: Hallandale, FL :
Mitchell Lane Publishers, [2018]

Series: Meet the Leaders

Library bound ISBN: 9781680202243

eBook ISBN: 9781680202250

EZ readers is an imprint of
Mitchell Lane Publishers

Photo credits: Cover, pp. 4-5, 8-9, 10-11, 12-13, 14-15, 16-17, 18-19, 20-21 Getty Images, pp. 6-7 Jefferson County Sherriff Dept., p. 22 freepik.com

Contents

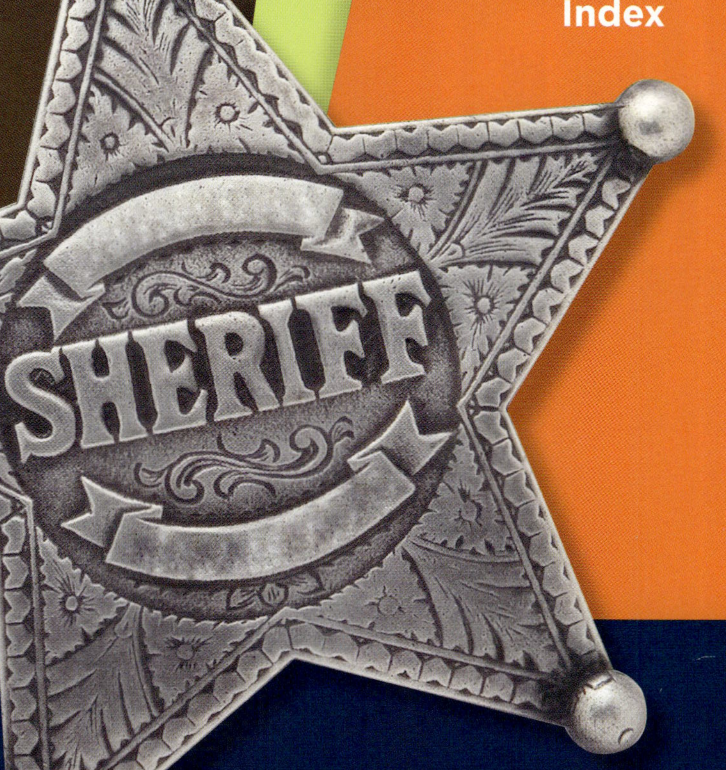

SHERIFF

Today I met our sheriff.

People **vote** for sheriffs.

SHERIFF
SHERIFF

The sheriff wears a **uniform.**

He wears a **badge**.

MOTOROLA
Commander II
BALTIMORE CITY
HERIF

He drives a sheriff's **car.**

SHERIFF

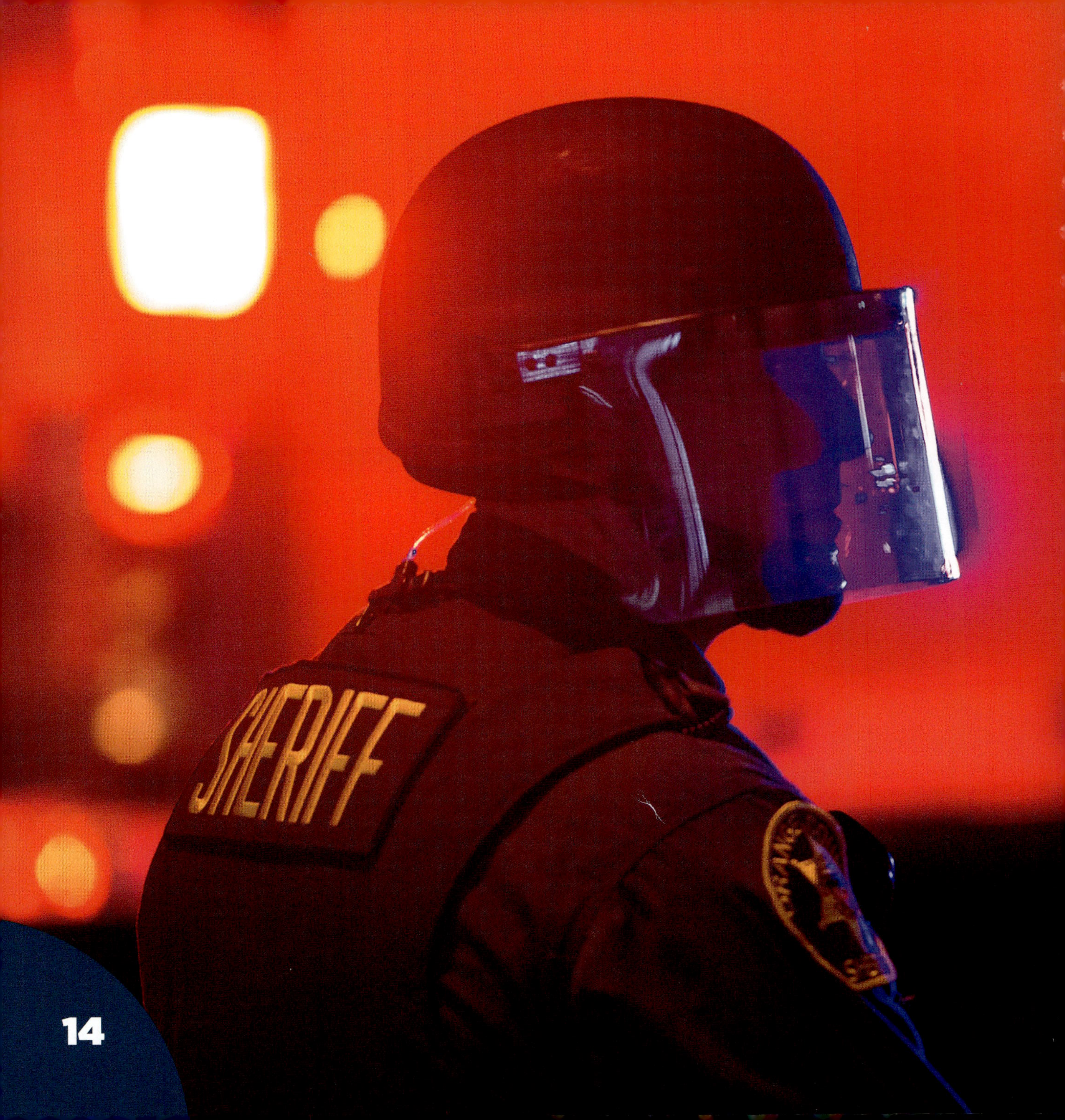
SHERIFF

Sheriffs make sure **laws** are followed.

Sheriffs keep people safe.

They also keep our roads safe.

PAUSE
BRIGHT
VOLUME
Z
M
T
W

SHERIFF
SHERIFF
SHERIFF

Maybe one day,
I will be a sheriff!

Picture Glossary

badge
A small object such as a tag, pin, or metal shield

car
A vehicle that has four wheels and an engine and is used for carrying passengers on roads

laws
A set of rules made by the government of a town, state, country, etc.

people
A group of men, women, and/or children

road
A hard, flat surface for vehicles, people, and animals to travel on

safe
Not in danger

uniform
A special kind of clothing that is worn by all the members of a group or organization

vote
To make an official choice for or against someone or something

Did you know?

- The sheriff is the chief officer in a county. A county is bigger than a city. A city is part of a county.
- Sheriffs are chosen in a county election.
- Sheriff Zena Stephens on page seven is the first ever black female sheriff in Texas.
- Sheriffs take an oath. They promise not to break laws.
- The officers who help the sheriff are called deputy sheriffs.
- Sheriffs do some of the same jobs as police officers. Both arrest people who break the law.
- Sheriffs also run the county jail.

Index